THE SCIENCE BEHIND
MERMAIDS, WEREWOLVES, AND BIGFOOT

JOY LIN AND VIOLET TOBACCO

Gareth Stevens
PUBLISHING

Please visit our website,
www.garethstevens.com.
For a free color catalog of all
our high-quality books, call
toll free 1-800-542-2595 or
fax 1-877-542-2596.

Published in 2025 by
Gareth Stevens Publishing
2544 Clinton St.
Buffalo, NY 14224

First published in Great Britain in 2021 by Wayland
Text © Joy Lin, 2021
Artwork and design © Hodder and Stoughton, 2021

Editors: Elise Short and Grace Glendinning
Designer: Peter Scoulding
Illustration: Violet Tobacco

Cataloging-in-Publication Data

Names: Lin, Joy, author. | Tobacco, Violet, illustrator.
Title: The science behind mermaids, werewolves, and bigfoot /
  by Joy Lin, illustrated by Violet Tobacco.
Description: New York : Gareth Stevens Publishing, 2025. |
  Series: Monster science | Includes glossary and index.
Identifiers: ISBN 9781538294239 (pbk.) | ISBN 9781538294246 (library bound) |
  ISBN 9781538294253 (ebook)
Subjects: LCSH: Mermaids--Juvenile literature. | Werewolves--Juvenile literature. |
  Sasquatch--Juvenile literature. | Science--Juvenile literature.
Classification: LCC GR910.L56 2025 | DDC 398.21--dc23

Printed in the United States of America

CPSIA compliance information: Batch #CSGS25: For further information contact Gareth Stevens at 1-800-542-2595.

 Find us on

CONTENTS

INTRODUCTION

Are you curious about mermaids, human from the waist up and fish from the waist down? Are you wary of the werewolf – human by day, angry wolf by moonlit night? Are you baffled by Bigfoot – part human, part ape?

If you've ever wondered whether any of these creatures are scientifically possible, you've come to the right place. This book is here to help you. By sorting truth from myth and examining the scientific facts, you'll discover whether any of these beings could exist and what chance you might have of ever coming face-to-face with one of them.

Meet the Monsters

You probably don't think of mermaids

as monsters, but stories about them date way back to ancient Greece, and they aren't pretty.

Legends tell of creatures called sirens that were vicious half-fish, half-women. Said to be daughters of the sea god, their singing was so beautiful that it lured sailors to steer their ships onto jagged rocks, where sirens lay in wait. Shipwrecks were regular occurrences, and many people believed that dreadful, vengeful monsters lurked beneath the oceans. These monsters helped to explain why storms could whip up from nowhere and swallow ships whole. The sailors at the time all knew the legend of the evil sirens, and many reported seeing them. But what did they really see?

Over the years, mermaids have had a change of image. These days you'll find them in romantic stories, living in kingdoms under the sea and flitting about in fancy swimsuits made of seashells. But, nice or nasty, can a half-fish, half-human creature really exist and appear in our world?

Werewolves are definitely terrifying, but they're fascinating at the same time. A film called *The Wolf Man* made them popular in the twentieth century and inspired a lot of popular spin-offs. Before that, werewolf stories in the nineteenth century were fueled by Jo-Jo the Dog-faced Boy, who was part of American showman P.T. Barnum's traveling circus.

But the legend of the werewolf goes back much farther than that. According to the ancient Greeks, King Lycaon was turned into a wolf by Zeus, king of the gods, as punishment for serving him human meat as an offering. Across Europe in the Middle Ages (fifth to fifteenth centuries), many men were tried, convicted, and executed after confessing that they were werewolves.

Even today, stories of werewolves are told around the world, but should you be worried? Is it scientifically possible for one creature to turn into another? And what's so special about the light of the moon?

When it comes to Bigfoot, this creature is shrouded in mystery. According to some theories, it is another species of human, in the same way a greyhound and a Chihuahua are two different species of dog. Reported sightings suggest that Bigfoot is a tall, hairy, ape-like animal that walks on two legs, the way humans do. It doesn't speak our languages, and it tends to run as soon as we approach it. Could Bigfoot be our distant cousin? And with similar sightings around the world, could Bigfoot be linked to the Yeti, the legendary abominable snowman — reportedly similar to Bigfoot, except with white hair?

We'll find out the answers to all these questions together.

Feeling curious? Then let's get started ...

Mermaids

Do you think of a mermaid as the beautiful creature with long, wavy hair, a seashell bikini, the voice of an angel, and the tail of a fish from the belly button down? Or as the dangerous kind of creature who uses her eerie singing voice to lure sailors to their doom? And would you say she is a human with a fish tail or a fish with a human body and head? Either way, a mermaid is a fascinating creature. The question is: does the fish–human combination make actual scientific sense?

Skin and Scales

Let's start with the skin-and-scales combination and how that might work.

So, what are scales? Just as human nails protect our fingertips, the hard scales on a fish protect its skin. Arranged in an overlapping pattern, they form a layer that makes predator or parasite attacks more difficult. Scales also reduce water resistance when the fish is swimming and allow it to be fast and flexible in the water.

With this in mind, how would the half-and-half combo work for a mermaid? If only half of a mermaid's body is covered in scales, the soft skin of the human half would be vulnerable to attack, injury, and infection. So a mermaid would probably be quite a sickly creature, not the dazzling one you'd expect.

The mix of skin and scales would also mean part of her would be quick in water and the other half would drag as water passes over the different textures of her body. Not the sleekest of swimmers! So much for grace and beauty...

A vital question: breathing

Next in the half-fish, half-human puzzle, we have the very important question of breathing. Both fish and humans need oxygen in order to survive, but humans breathe in air while fish breathe in water.

Human lungs can extract oxygen from air easily. So the mermaid could breathe in oxygen through her lungs (if she has them), but only when her head's out of the water. We've all tried at some point to stay underwater for as long as possible. The world record is 30 minutes, but the average for a healthy person is only 2 minutes! Are all mermaids secret world-record holders for holding their breath, then?

Even if they are, to come up for oxygen every 30 minutes would make life quite difficult! Could you hold a conversation with your pet crab if you had to rise to the surface all the time?

A GULP OF OXYGEN

When a fish opens its mouth, water enters its body. The water then passes through to the gills, where oxygen is extracted. Then the water is pushed back out of the body. As long as the oxygen level in a fish's blood is lower than the oxygen level in the water, oxygen will move from the water to the fish's bloodstream.

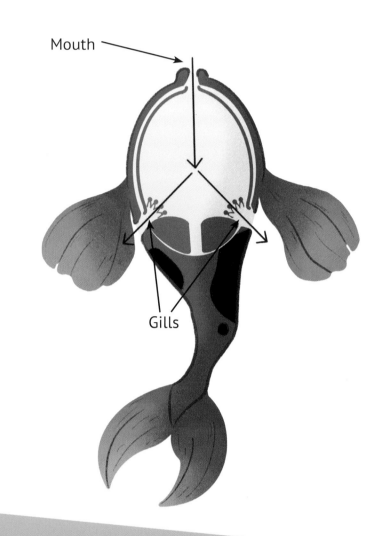

Mouth

Gills

THE GREAT OXYGEN EXCHANGE

The fish's breathing process is especially efficient because the blood passing through the gills is pumped in the opposite direction to the water flowing out of them, a process called countercurrent exchange. More contact between water and blood means more oxygen passing into the bloodstream. To get your head around this idea, imagine you're running in the opposite direction to a parade. Facing this direction, you can high-five loads more people than if you're running in the same direction as the parade.

Blood flowing in the opposite direction to the water has just the same effect; it can take up much more oxygen.

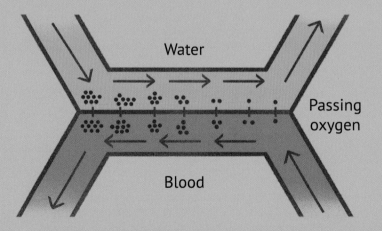

Water

Passing oxygen

Blood

Could a mermaid take in water through her mouth and then pass it out through gills? Come to think of it, have you ever seen a mermaid depicted with gills?

THE OXYGEN BUS

Once the blood is oxygenated, it courses through the fish's body to distribute oxygen wherever it is needed, a bit like a bus full of homeward-bound grammar school children being let off at various stops along the route. Once the bus is empty again, it goes back to pick up more children. The cycle, known as the circulatory system, continues...

All of this happens at a speed of almost 3 feet (1 meter) per second!

So, does a mermaid have a fish's circulatory system in the bottom half of her body and a human's in the top?

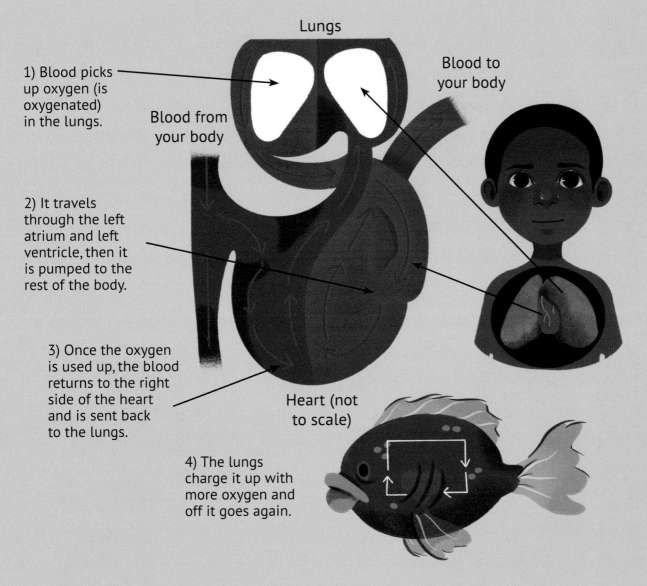

Lungs

1) Blood picks up oxygen (is oxygenated) in the lungs.

Blood to your body

Blood from your body

2) It travels through the left atrium and left ventricle, then it is pumped to the rest of the body.

3) Once the oxygen is used up, the blood returns to the right side of the heart and is sent back to the lungs.

Heart (not to scale)

4) The lungs charge it up with more oxygen and off it goes again.

It seems unlikely the two systems would work well together. This half-fish, half-human situation sure seems complicated and not really possible scientifically... but let's consider one last thing in the mermaid question.

Half hot, half cold?

Have you considered the fact that fish are cold-blooded creatures, while humans are mammals, which means we're warm-blooded? A fish's body temperature depends on the water temperature it's swimming in. This means that it requires less energy to maintain its body temperature because the water does the job.

However, a warm-blooded animal, such as a human, regulates its temperature internally and uses up a lot more energy to do so. This all works very well on land when humans are surrounded by air, but when in water, it's a whole different story!

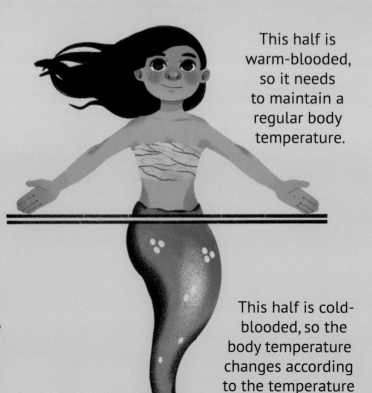

This half is warm-blooded, so it needs to maintain a regular body temperature.

This half is cold-blooded, so the body temperature changes according to the temperature of its surroundings.

Too hot, too cold?

First thing is, water transmits heat much better than air, and this has a huge effect on the human body. If the water is too hot, the body will overheat, causing HYPERthermia. If the water is too cold, the body will develop HYPOthermia. Both can cause confusion, increased heart rate, and in extreme cases, death.

The best water temperature for a human is around 77–80°F (25–27°C). These temperatures are only found in certain areas of the world's oceans, and only at the surface of the water, so a mermaid would not be able to swim very deep. No underwater kingdoms for mermaids, then. And if they have to swim near the surface to survive, how have they managed to elude us for so long?

It seems safe to say that, based on all the science principles we've covered so far, the half-fish, half-human combination is far from a winning one. So how can we explain historic sightings of mermaids? Maybe these mermaids were something different altogether...

THE DREAMY DUGONG

Dugong

Researchers now know that mermaid sightings were in fact neither fish nor human. The sea creature frequently mistaken for a mermaid is actually a mammal called a dugong, classified under the species order Sirenia. Spot the likeness? No, we can't either.

Measuring up to 1 foot (3 m) long, with a tail like a dolphin's, and weighing up to a scale-busting 2,200 pounds (1,000 kg), if a dugong really was our mermaid, you might be forgiven for calling it a monster. In reality, its personality is anything but monstrous.

Dugongs are sometimes called sea cows, though they're actually related to elephants. They drift about sleepily while chomping on sea grass and holding their breath underwater for up to 8 minutes. They can be found in the shallow waters of Indo-Pacific Asia.

SEASICK SAILORS

So how did sailors mistake dugongs (and their Caribbean cousins, the manatees) for mermaids?

Well, before fridges were invented, the fresh water on board a ship would go bad quickly. Within a month it would have turned slimy. Drinking sea water wasn't an option — the salt would make the sailors sick. So they solved the problem by mixing water with rum to make "grog." Adding alcohol to water keeps it from spoiling, but it also meant the sailors would be slightly drunk all the time.

With no fresh fruit on board, many sailors also suffered from scurvy, a disease that could leave sailors exhausted and delirious, making their stories even more unreliable. Maybe the tales of mermaids first surfaced because sailors — tired, drunk, and sick — saw unfamiliar sea creatures like dugongs in the distance, flopping around near the surface of the water, surrounded by sea grass. Perhaps they mistook them for sunbathing half-women with long, wavy hair dancing in the ocean?

13

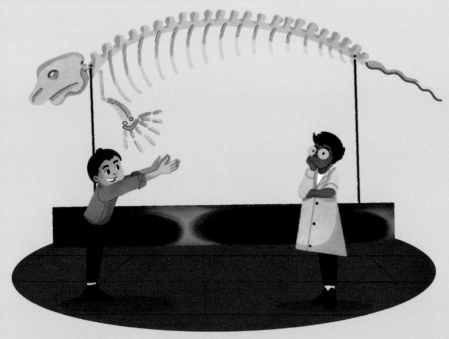

A HANDY SKELETON

Or maybe it was the dugong's skeleton that sparked the mermaid connection?

As well as its fishy tail, the dugong has flippers roughly where we have arms. The bones of the flippers look quite like human arm bones, with elbows and five fingers. A skeleton with human hands *and* a tail? Now that does sound rather like a mermaid.

DWINDLING DUGONGS

Sadly, dugong numbers are dwindling. In the past they've been hunted. People ate their meat and used oil from their bodies to protect boats, and in Japan they used to carve dugong ribs into intricate sculptures.

Today, thankfully, they are a protected species in many parts of the world, but like lots of sea creatures, they're still under threat from climate change and human activity in the sea.

So a "mermaid" isn't the evil woman who'll lure a sailor to crash on the rocks, and she isn't the singing girl with the seashell swimsuit. She's something altogether different and beautiful in its own way. Spotting a dugong is as rare and amazing as spotting a real mermaid — maybe you'll be so lucky one day!

MERMAID SIGHTINGS: not what you were thinking, but not impossible!

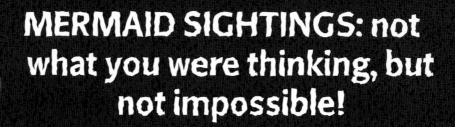

Werewolves

Stories of werewolves are terrifying. They tell of people who turn into wolves when there is a full moon, becoming stronger and faster than any human. They can only be defeated by being burned at the stake or attacked with a weapon made of silver. Most terrifying of all, according to legend, is that any person bitten by a werewolf will turn into one, too, shedding their clothes at the next full moon, eager to hunt their first prey...

But hang on a minute, why would the full moon have such an effect? After all, isn't moonlight just a weak reflection of sunlight?

LIGHT SIDE OF THE MOON

A full moon occurs when the moon is directly opposite the sun, with Earth right in the middle.

Moonlight given off by the moon at night is actually just reflected sunlight. Because of the roughness of the moon's surface, however, only about 11 percent of sunlight is reflected back to Earth. Sunlight and moonlight, then, are made up of the same spectrum of visible light — UV (ultraviolet) light and infrared light; it's just that the sun's is more intense.

So, if sunlight and moonlight are the same thing, why doesn't sunlight have a *stronger* effect on werewolves? Is it the reflection itself that causes the supernatural reaction? If so, then surely all an "infected" person would have to do to avoid the transformation would be to hide in a windowless room at nighttime … right?

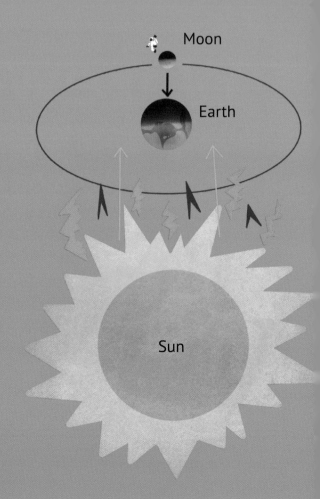

Moon

Earth

Sun

Moon's gravitational pull

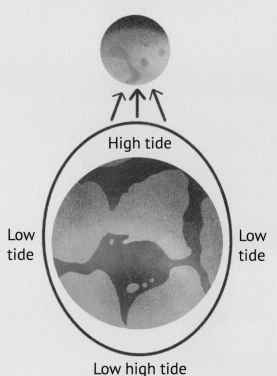

High tide

Low tide

Low tide

Low high tide

BOUNCING ON THE MOON

Actually, there *is* something special about the moon. It's not just a shining orb in the night sky. It has an effect on our lives down on Earth.

You may have heard of gravity, the force that attracts objects toward one another and keeps us grounded on Earth. The reason you or any other object on Earth doesn't float off into space is due to Earth's gravitational pull on us.

The moon also exerts gravitational pull on us, but it is much weaker than Earth's. Despite this, it's still strong enough to have visible effects on Earth in the form of tides. The moon's gravity literally pulls the water level up on the side it's closest to!

The opposite side of Earth will have a "low high tide" at this time because Earth, too, is being pulled toward the moon. The areas between the two high tides will have low tides as the water is pulled away.

LION LIGHT

So can the moon have a similar effect on people?
Could a full moon cause any of us to start howling and sprouting fur?

Since human bodies are about 60 percent water, some people say that when the moon is closer to Earth it can affect our behavior as well as the ocean's. Throughout history, there have been reports of increased crime rates and mental health problems during a full moon. However, scientific studies have concluded that a full moon's pull doesn't have any impact on our behavior. In fact, it's been noted that a mosquito sucking blood from your arm exerts more gravitational force on you than the moon does!

In parts of Africa, however, lion attacks on humans definitely spike in the days right after a full moon. The reason for the lions' behavior is easily explained — and, sadly, there's nothing magical about it. On moonlit nights, Earth is brighter. Humans (and other prey) can see an attacker more easily, and that allows them more time to run. Lions have to lie low during this time. In the days after a full moon, lions are ravenous, so attacks on humans increase.

As for reports of changes in human behavior, historically, before electricity provided us with a 24-hour light source, the brightness of the full moon used to keep people awake. Lack of sleep can make existing conditions worse, causing anxiety and probably affecting people's behavior.

Today, with lights available at the flick of a switch and blackout curtains to stop unwanted brightness from waking us up, a full moon no longer signals sleep deprivation, so the whole idea that people might act differently — or shape-shift into a wolf — during a full moon, is a thing of the past.

Skinny Werewolf

Moonlight or no moonlight, what if you *could* transform into a wolf? Well, the scientific law of conservation of mass states that mass (the weightiness of an object) cannot be created or destroyed. If you play with a piece of clay, you can turn it into lots of different shapes, but the clay should still have the same mass whether it ends up looking like a ball or a long, thin snake. It's the same for a werewolf: its mass should stay the same before and after the transformation. So if a skinny human were to transform into a werewolf, he'd become ... a very skinny werewolf.

It's safe to say quite a few of the werewolves running around would be rather tiny, not even as big as regular wolves; did you know the largest wolf on record weighed over 220 lbs (100 kg)?

Pros and Cons

Just for a moment, suppose you could be a wolf; there are some definite advantages. Wolves have excellent eyesight and great hearing, and their sense of smell is 100 times better than a human's. Imagine being able to sniff out your dinner when you're just setting off for home from school! On a clear day, a wolf can smell its prey from 1.7 miles (2.8 km) away.

Those all seem like handy traits to have, but this all comes with a wolf's unavoidable instinct to use its bone-crushing teeth and its rough tongue to rip into uncooked flesh and pull it off the bone. Ugh!

WOLFING IT DOWN

Another fascinating thing about wolves is that they can survive for weeks without food if they have to. Then, when the opportunity presents itself, they'll put away over 22 lbs (10 kg) of meat in one sitting! If that wolf happens to be of the werewolf variety, imagine how he's going to feel the next day. Back in human form, he'd be having serious tummy trouble.

A human stomach can't even hold one-third of the amount eaten by a wolf before it's full to bursting. With so much raw meat inside a human's tummy, it would surely cause a ruptured stomach the moment the werewolf changed back.

Even in the unlikely event that the werewolf doesn't overeat, the contents of its undigested prey — including fur, bones, guts, and even poo (ew!) — would seriously mess up a human stomach.

PEEING FREELY

Another awkward issue is that wolves are very territorial. Humans use walls and fences to mark out their property, but wolves use something else: their own strong-smelling pee. Yes, they pee everywhere to warn others to stay out of their territory. Once a werewolf wakes up as a human again, there'd be lots of cleaning up to do!

FAIRLY HAIRY

But what about Jo-Jo the Dog-Faced Boy from the beginning of the book? He didn't burst or pee on himself. Isn't he proof that werewolves exist?

Yes, Jo-Jo could talk and was covered in fur, but there's no suggestion that he ever *transformed* from hairy to smooth (and back), and there's certainly no need to be afraid of anyone who just happens to have an unusually hairy face. Jo-Jo's dad was also covered in hair, and it seems likely they both had a condition called generalized hypertrichosis (also known as werewolf syndrome). The condition is genetic, so it can be passed down from one generation to the next.

Apart from a few places, such as the soles of our feet, the palms of our hands, and our eyelids and lips, human bodies have hair or hair follicles just about everywhere. Genes control the variety of human hair color and thickness, which is different from one person to the next. In generalized hypertrichosis, excessive hair grows all over the body because of a difference in the hair-controlling genes.

Jo-Jo wasn't really a werewolf. His howling was just an act. In fact, another common effect of hypertrichosis is that sufferers hardly have any teeth, and their voices are soft and smooth. Not very wolf-like at all!

WEREWOLF HUNTS

Then there were the prisoners in the Middle Ages who *confessed* to being werewolves. Surely that's proof that the creatures existed?

Well, it seems some of them were probably genuine murderers trying to excuse their bad behavior. Other confessions may have simply been forced lies, told while the accused was being tortured.

There are still some accounts that can't be explained, but it could be because people accused of being werewolves were often captured and given a sort of trial with fake witnesses and no real chance to prove their innocence — just as accused witches were. Many innocent people were tragically executed as "werewolves" by the most effective means legend claimed would kill the magical beasts: burning them at the stake.

Saved by Silver

According to folklore, burning isn't the only way you can defeat a werewolf. These super-fast, super-strong monsters can also be stopped with a silver bullet, as they are said to be deathly allergic to silver.

Suppose you had a silver bullet, and the appropriate weapon to fire it. What are the odds you'd be able to shoot the werewolf before it attacked? So maybe another method of using silver is the better option?

Being an awesome conductor that transmits heat easily, silver is found in lots of places, from most electronic devices to windows and light bulbs. It's also a well-known purifier, able to kill disease-carrying bacteria, viruses, microorganisms, and fungii. The ancient Greeks, Romans, and Egyptians used silver to purify their water, and pioneers in the U.S. dropped a silver dollar into their water supply to keep it fresh. Even today in the U.S., silver is used to filter and purify drinking water supplies. If werewolves get thirsty in the U.S., they're in a world of trouble! Filtered water and plain tap water both have traces of wolf-killing silver.

In reality it seems highly unlikely that werewolves have ever existed or that you'd ever come into contact with one. If you did, however, at least you know that as long as you keep the right bottle of water with you at all times, you can just spray that

werewolf in the face when he tries to attack and get rid of him once and for all.

WEREWOLF INFESTATION: NOT POSSIBLE!

Bigfoot

Imagine you and your family are driving along a dark country road at night. Suddenly, a tire blows and you're forced to pull onto the shoulder. Once the tire is fixed, the engine roars to life, the lights flip on, and there, caught in the headlights, is an enormous creature. It stands a monumental 10 feet (3 m) tall — a cross between an ape and a man, with reddish-brown matted fur all over its body. It looks at you, then saunters off into the trees …

Hairy Hominids

You've just witnessed a pretty spectacular Bigfoot sighting. Hairy hominids (or primates) like this one lurk in just about every major culture — in legends at least.

North America has Bigfoot.
In the Himalayas there's the Yeti.
Australia has the Yowie.
In South America there's the Mapinguari.
In China it's the Yeren.
In India there's the Mande Barung.

Each creature may also be known by a variety of names within each country! That's a lot of hairy hominids.

It was only in 1958, when super-large footprints were discovered in California, that Bigfoot got its name. Before that, it was generally called a Sasquatch, which means "wild man" in a Native American language. Whatever their origins, stories of these creatures are so fascinating that some researchers today still dedicate their lives to proving that they're true. But can there possibly be another species of primate on Earth that we have no real knowledge of? And could *you* ever spot one?

Caught on Camera

In the following few decades after the footprints were discovered in California, there were suddenly lots more reported sightings.

Some people supposedly captured Bigfoot on film; others made sound recordings. Even the Federal Bureau of Investigation (FBI) got involved. It compiled a file on Bigfoot. If the FBI was taking Bigfoot seriously, it must have believed it could exist!

Let's see if science can help us work out whether they were right.

Six-Million-Year Journey

First, we'll need to go back six million years, to the time when the human lineage first split from chimpanzees, our closest known relatives. One of the earliest of these ancestors is called *Orrorin tugenensis*. Nicknamed Millennium Man, it was the size of a chimpanzee and had small teeth with thick enamel, similar to humans today. Fossil evidence has led scientists to believe that they climbed trees but also probably walked upright with two legs on the ground (we call that bipedalism).

Leap forward three million years — that's the time it took the Millennium Man to evolve into an early human, *Australopithecus*. This species from eastern Africa had a similar brain size, diet, and biology to apes and walked on two legs. Some of its features and bones were beginning to appear human-like.

Move on another million years or so — still two million years ago — and a new species had evolved a larger brain and hands for finer movements but still had longer, ape-like arms. This species of early humans is called *Homo habilis*.

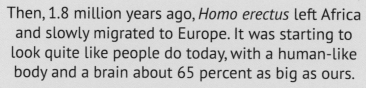

Then, 1.8 million years ago, *Homo erectus* left Africa and slowly migrated to Europe. It was starting to look quite like people do today, with a human-like body and a brain about 65 percent as big as ours.

About half a million years ago, Neanderthals, with slightly *larger* brains than today's humans, appeared. It is thought that their brains were larger because they had larger eyes than modern humans. They needed the larger eyes because they lived high up in the mountains, where there's little sunlight during long, dark winters. Processing information from their eyes took up a lot of brain space, which explains their brain size.

Then, roughly 200,000 years ago, *Homo sapiens* emerged in Africa. It took around 160,000 years for them to make it to Europe, where they arrived 40,000 years ago.

The height of our ancestors steadily increased over those six million years, but if the Sasquatch is related to us, it would mean that our ancestors' height went from 65 inches (165 cm) as Neanderthals to up to 118 inches (300 cm) as Bigfoot. Unfortunately, that doesn't match up with fossil records.

DISTANT COUSINS?

Though the Yeti and Bigfoot have origins half a world apart — Bigfoot sightings have mainly been in warmer climates such as the woods or swamps of North America, while the Yeti supposedly lives in the Himalayan mountains of South Asia — some scientists think they may have evolved from a single species, a different type of primate that existed 1.9 million years ago: Gigantopithecus.

Gentle Giants

Gigantopithecus was a bear-sized ape, descended from the same ape ancestors as we are. While we're closely related to chimpanzees, it was closer in type to orangutans. Gigantopithecus was larger than a gorilla and had teeth similar to human teeth — which sounds close to reports about both Yeti and Bigfoot. If we use what we know about orangutans to consider the possibility of a modern-day, human-like descendent of Gigantopithecus, we can see why some scientists are drawn to this idea.

Most primates live in packs, but the orangutan is a solitary animal that only mixes with others when it wants to mate and have babies. Hmmm, this solitary behavior sounds an awful lot like the descriptions of Bigfoot and Yeti. Also, the orangutan is curious and intelligent — reports suggest the same is true of Bigfoot and Yeti. So it sounds believable, but what about scientifically possible?

Too Big to Eat Roots

Scientists believe that Gigantopithecus died out between 300,000 and 100,000 years ago as a result of a temperature drop that transformed its forest habitat and caused the trees to die. In order to survive, Gigantopithecus needed to adapt its diet from mainly fruit (or possibly bamboo) to mainly grass, roots, and leaves.

Being huge, whatever Gigantopithecus ate, it needed an awful lot of it. Big animals also tend to have fewer babies. If they can't find enough food, reproduction is difficult and so is adapting to their new environment. Stretching up to 10 feet (3 m) tall and weighing over 660 lb (300 kg), it seems highly likely that, for Gigantopithecus, size was its downfall.

TALKING TEETH

Gigantopithecus itself wasn't discovered until 1935, after a paleontologist bought some "dragon's teeth" from a Chinese medicine shop and realized they belonged to some unknown giant, human-like creature. More of these huge teeth and fragments of a heavy jawbone were soon discovered. From the locations of the findings it was easy to work out where the creature lived, but the teeth also told a story.

By looking at how the teeth had worn down, some scientists suggested that the animal ate mostly bamboo, and by analyzing chemicals found on the tooth enamel, others could trace the plants and fruits it most likely ate.

The trouble is, without seeing more of the skeleton, we can't really know whether Gigantopithecus walked on two legs, like Bigfoot and the Yeti, or used its knuckles, more like a gorilla.

CROSSING CONTINENTS

But did Gigantopithecus really die out, or is it possible that the creature carried on living quietly in the depths of the forest, resurfacing as Bigfoot or the Yeti?

Gigantopithecus remains suggest that the creature roamed all over Southeast Asia, so perhaps there could be a connection with the Yeti. Bigfoot, on the other hand, originates from a completely different continent. There is no evidence of a different primate evolving in the Americas, so the only way it could have reached the continent would have been during an ice age, when a bridge formed between Asia and the far north of North America, and most scientists think that's unlikely.

Bigfoot or Bambi?

The biggest problem with the story of Bigfoot, however, is that there is no concrete evidence to prove it exists. There are no bone, hair, or tissue samples. In 1975, the FBI investigated a hair sample attached to a piece of skin, thinking it might belong to Bigfoot. The result? It came from a member of the deer family! Meanwhile, hairs from a supposed Yeti have been linked to a rare type of brown bear — not a primate at all.

Bigfeet?

Of course, if Bigfoot was real, you wouldn't just see one lone creature wandering the countryside. Individual creatures couldn't survive for millennia all on their own. It takes at least one male and one female primate to create a baby, and for a species to survive and thrive, there would need to be many more. (Should we call them Bigfeet?) Over generations, a small population would need to increase to survive, so there should be plenty of Bigfeet to spot, whether or not they all live together in a pack.

And today we have the technology to spot them, even in the dark or from very far away. All objects give off a level of infrared radiation. Body heat shows up a different color on a thermal camera, day or night, whatever the weather, so Bigfoot really shouldn't have anywhere to hide.

PLENTY MORE FISH...

It's not impossible for a new species to be discovered, however. We're all familiar with the giant panda today, but until 1869, no Westerner had ever seen one. Westerners didn't find out about mountain gorillas, either, until 1902! It's estimated that roughly 8.7 million different life-forms exist on Earth (most of them are insects). Of those, it's likely that less than a quarter have been identified!

If you really want to discover new species, the best place to search is a tropical forest or, even better, under the sea. You may not find a giant — larger creatures are so much easier to spot and identify with today's technology — but you might uncover something smaller. A new invertebrate, perhaps?

IT'S FAKE!

But what about all those Bigfoot reports, videos, and sound recordings? Some of them must be real, surely? Sadly, it turned out that even the footprints that gave Bigfoot its name in the 1950s were created as a prank! If you look at Bigfoot video recordings you'll see the creature is usually either vague and distant, or clearly a person in a gorilla suit. Even sound recordings can be manipulated with the help of computer technology. Evidence is all too easy to fake.

According to scientific thinking, however, you can only prove that a creature does exist, not that it doesn't. And some scientists and scholars still firmly believe in Bigfoot in spite of all the pranksters. So keep your eyes peeled ... you never know what you might find.

BIGFOOT SIGHTINGS: UNLIKELY, BUT NOT IMPOSSIBLE

GLOSSARY

atrium the upper chamber of each half of the heart

bloodstream the blood that flows around a body

circulatory system the system that transports blood around the body, including the heart and blood vessels

climate change changes in Earth's climate, especially to do with the gradual rise in temperature caused by high levels of carbon dioxide and other gases

cold-blooded animals whose body temperature changes according to the surrounding temperature

conductor a substance that heat or electricity can pass through or along

evolve to change and develop over a period of time

execute to kill as punishment for a serious crime

fossil the hard remains of a prehistoric animal or plant that are found inside a rock

genetic to do with genes

gravitational pull attraction caused by gravity

hominid any primate of the Hominidae family, which includes modern humans (*Homo sapiens*)

hyperthermia a condition where the body has a very high fever and temperature

hypothermia a condition where the body temperature becomes dangerously low because of being in extreme cold for a long time

infrared camera a camera that creates an image using infrared radiation

legend a very old and well-known story that may or may not be true

mass in physics, the amount of physical matter belonging to an object

myth a story that was made up in the past to explain religious beliefs or customs

oxygenate to mix or dissolve oxygen into something

paleontologist someone who studies prehistoric life forms through the study of fossils

parasite a small animal or plant that lives on or inside a bigger animal or plant, from which it gets its food

predator an animal that kills and eats other animals

prey animals that are hunted and killed for food

primate member of the group of mammals that includes humans, monkeys, and apes

scurvy a disease caused by a lack of vitamin C, which particularly affected sailors until the end of the 18th century

sea cow a large, vegetarian sea mammal with a cigar-shaped body, blunt snout, mobile lips, and forelimbs like flippers

shape-shift to change shape at will or under certain conditions

siren a sea nymph from Greek mythology who used her singing to lure sailors to destruction on rocks

species a group of plants or animals that share the same main characteristics and are able to breed with each other

spectrum a range of something

territorial behavior around the ownership of an area and the defense of it from others

tides the regular change in the level of the ocean on the shore

ultraviolet (UV) light the part of the electromagnetic spectrum with wavelengths shorter than light but longer than X-rays

ventricle part of the heart that pumps blood to the arteries

warm-blooded animals that have a constant body temperature that is usually higher than the temperature of their surroundings

water resistance a type of force that uses friction to slow things down that are moving through water

FURTHER INFORMATION

FURTHER FREAKY SCIENCE READING:

Cause, Effect and Chaos! In the Animal Kingdom
by Paul Mason
(Wayland, 2020)

A Question of Science: Why Can't Penguins Fly?
And Other Questions About Animals
by Anna Claybourne
(Wayland, 2020)

The *Body Bits* series, including the following
fantastic books:
Astounding Animal Body Facts
Awesome Dinosaur Body Facts
Eye-Popping Plant Part Facts
Hair-Raising Human Body Facts
by Paul Mason
(Gareth Stevens, 2023)

Animals in Disguise
by Michael Bright
(Wayland, 2020)

PLACES TO SEE FREAKY SCIENCE UP CLOSE:

American Museum of Natural History
200 Central Park West
New York, NY 10024
https://www.amnh.org

National Museum of Natural History
10th Street and Constitution Avenue NW
Washington, DC 20560
https:/naturalhistory.si.edu

Natural History Museum
900 Exposition Boulevard
Los Angeles, CA 90007
https://nhm.org

Canada Museum of Nature
240 McLeod Street
Ottawa, ON K2P 2R1
https://nature.ca/en/

INDEX